Reduce and Reuse

Sally Hewitt

Crabtree Publishing Company
www.crabtreebooks.com

Crabtree Publishing Company
www.crabtreebooks.com

Author: Sally Hewitt
Editors: Jeremy Smith, Molly Aloian
Proofreaders: Adrianna Morganelli, Crystal Sikkens
Project editor: Robert Walker
Production coordinator: Margaret Amy Salter
Art director: Jonathan Hair
Design: Jason Anscomb
Prepress technician: Katherine Kantor

Activity pages development by Shakespeare Squared
www.shakespearesquared.com

Picture credits: Alamy: pages 6, 7 (bottom), 8, 10, 11, 18, 19, 21 (top right), 22, 23, 24; Corbis: page 14; Computers for Schools: page 17 (bottom); Freecycle: page 9 (top and bottom); Friends of Malawi Orphans: page 15; istockphoto: page 21 (top left); Shutterstock: OFC, pages 3, 7 (top), 9 (right), 12, 16, 17 (top); St Joseph's School: page 13; Trafalgar Infant & Junior School: pages 26-27; Wonga Beach School: page 20
Every attempt has been made to clear copyright. Should there be any inadvertent omission, please contact the publisher for rectification.

Library and Archives Canada Cataloguing in Publication

Hewitt, Sally, 1949-
    Reduce and reuse / Sally Hewitt.

(Green team)
Includes index.

ISBN 978-0-7787-4095-7 (bound).--ISBN 978-0-7787-4102-2 (pbk.)

    1. Waste minimization--Juvenile literature. 2. Salvage (Waste, etc.)--Juvenile literature. 3. Recycling (Waste, etc.)--Juvenile literature. I. Title. II. Series: Hewitt, Sally, 1949- . Green team.

TD793.9.H49 2008   j363.72'82   C2008-903489-9

Library of Congress Cataloging-in-Publication Data

Hewitt, Sally, 1949-
  Reduce and reuse / Sally Hewitt.
    p. cm. -- (Green team)
  Includes index.
  ISBN-13: 978-0-7787-4102-2 (pbk. : alk. paper)
  ISBN-10: 0-7787-4102-8 (pbk. : alk. paper)
  ISBN-13: 978-0-7787-4095-7 (reinforced library binding : alk. paper)
  ISBN-10: 0-7787-4095-1 (reinforced library binding : alk. paper)
  1. Waste minimization--Juvenile literature. 2. Salvage (Waste, etc.)--Juvenile literature. 3. Recycling (Waste, etc.)--Juvenile literature.
I. Title. II. Series.
  TD793.9.H49 2009
  363.72'82--dc22
                                        2008023287

Crabtree Publishing Company

www.crabtreebooks.com   1-800-387-7650

Published in Canada
Crabtree Publishing
616 Welland Ave.
St. Catharines, Ontario
L2M 5V6

Published in the United States
Crabtree Publishing
PMB16A
350 Fifth Ave., Suite 3308
New York, NY 10118

Contents

Going to waste

Natural resources such as wood, metals, oil, and gas are used to make all kinds of things we use every day. We often throw these things away without a thought, creating waste that ends up in a variety of different places.

We all produce a vast amount of garbage every year. **Landfill** sites like the one above will rapidly fill up unless we start **reducing** the amount we throw away.

Where does it go?

Litter

Some waste is thrown away carelessly and lies around as litter. Litter looks bad, blocks up drains, and can be dangerous to animals and people.

Landfills

Large amounts of garbage are taken to holes in the ground called landfills.

Garbage can take years to break down. As waste breaks down, poison leaks into the soil. Poisonous gases escape into the air. These gases affect our climate by causing **global warming**. Landfill sites are also expensive to control and maintain.

Incinerators

Incinerators are big fires or furnaces where garbage is burned. They send smoke into the air and create ash that has to be disposed of.

Not all of this garbage needs to go into a landfill. Some of it could easily be recycled or **reused**.

Action!

Make a garbage diary.
Record what goes into the trash at home and in your classroom under these headings:

- Glass
- Paper and cardboard
- Plastic
- Food and garden waste
- Textiles
- Other

Too much garbage

Households, stores, and factories all produce garbage. Some garbage, such as food and paper, is **biodegradable**. This means it breaks down naturally over time and disappears. Other garbage, made of materials such as glass, metal, and plastic, is non-biodegradable, which means it stays around for hundreds of years.

Challenge!

You can help.
- Reduce means to make less.
- Reduce the garbage you throw away at home.
- Reduce the garbage your class throws away at school.

Do not drop litter on the ground. Find a public garbage can or take it home with you.

Make less garbage

To join the Green Team, one of the most useful things you can do is make less garbage. You can start when you go shopping.

Challenge!

Think before you buy something new.

Ask yourself:

Do I really need it?

Have I already got one?

Can I borrow one?

How many times will I use it?

Can I use something else instead?

How long will I be interested in it?

When you have answered all those questions, ask yourself, do I still want to buy it?

Throw away

People say we live in a 'throw-away society.' This means we use things and then throw them away, sometimes when they are still quite new. But you can change that. First of all, try not to buy so much!

Making a list helps you to buy exactly what you need. This way, you will not buy too much food or things you do not need that you will throw away without even using.

Freecycle

Cut down on what you throw away. The Freecycle Network was founded in May 2003 in Tuscan to help save desert landscapes from being taken over by landfill sites. Today, there are Freecycle groups all over the world. They try to keep usable things out of landfill sites by passing them on to someone who will use them. Their aim is to reduce the number of things we make and buy.

At this Freecycle event, everyone brought along items they did not want and other people took them home and reused them.

Do not throw out things you do not want anymore.

• Hold a sale and give the money you make to an environmental charity.

• Join an organization such as Freecycle and give usable items away.

Pete   Jack

Jack's feet will grow and his roller blades will soon be too small for him. He can borrow a pair from his older brother Pete, and pass his onto someone else when they are too small for him. That way, he will make less garbage than if he buys a new pair.

Packaging and wrapping

Most of the garbage we throw away is packaging. Reducing the amount of packaging we bring into our homes and schools will help to reduce waste.

Food is one of the most packaged items we buy. Packaging makes the food more expensive, and leads to more litter (above right).

Food packaging

Food packaging helps to preserve, protect, and keep food fresh. A lot of the packaging is not necessary and can create litter that does not rot away.

Learn to cook

Precooked meals come in a lot of packaging. Cooking from fresh ingredients saves packaging and is usually a healthier choice.

School supplies

School supplies arrive in all kinds of packaging. Cardboard and paper are biodegradable and recyclable, but styrofoam cups and bubble wrap are not.

Learn how to cook using fresh ingredients. Not only does this create less waste but the food tastes better, too!

Challenge!

Make choices at the store.

- Choose one big packet, carton, or bottle instead of a lot of smaller ones.
- Buy concentrated cleaning products, which use less packaging.
- Do not buy products with several layers of packaging when one will do. If you do not think the packaging is necessary, challenge the store about its packaging policy by writing a letter or talking to the staff.

Case study— Reusing packaging

The Gene Rosenfield "Preserve Our Environment Leadership" Award is awarded every year to an American student for his or her efforts in protecting their environment. Sara Merando from Lakeland Regional High School, Wanaque, conserved paper by reusing paper that other students discarded. She collected used paper from the copy room for her use, as well. Sara was able to collect so much paper that she has not had to buy a notebook since her first year at high school.

Creative ideas

Other students at Sara's school reused their paper and packaging.

- They used shredded paper to make more paper (see page 19), which was then made into scrapbooks.
- Photo frames, notepaper cubes, and bags were just some of the other things the students made.

This girl is drawing on recycled paper, which was made from waste paper collected at her school.

This strong bag is made from recycled newspaper.

Books and magazines

When you have read a book, do not throw it away or leave it on a shelf getting dusty. There are all kinds of things you can do with books.

You do not have to buy a book to read it. You can borrow it from your local library.

Challenge!

Give old books a new life.

- Can you mend old or torn books?
- Can you lend books to friends?
- Can you sell books and use the money to buy more?
- Can you give your old books to schools or charities?

Libraries

Libraries are a great way of reusing books. If you are not a member of your local library, join it now. Instead of buying a new book, you can borrow some books and take them home to read. When you have finished, take the books back to the library and choose a new selection to read.

Magazines

Magazines and comics can be read again and again. Do not throw yours away. Find out if your doctor's office, hospital, or any other waiting room wants them and pass them on. Do not buy the same magazines or comics as your friends. Encourage each friend to buy a different one and share.

Case study— Read To Grow and Book Aid

If you do not want your books, there is always someone else who does. There are many schools all over the world who have very few books and urgently need more.

Read To Grow and Book Aid are charities that send books to schools in **developing countries**. St Joseph's Primary School in Glasgow, Scotland, is part of the Read to Grow plan. In 2004, they won the World Book Day Award for collecting the highest number of books.

⇒ Action!

Get your school to collect good quality used books.

- Choose a charity that will help you to send them to a school abroad.
- Use the Internet and email to make friends with children at the school.
- Maybe they will be able to help your school in return?

Children from St Joseph's are celebrating their award.

A school chart shows how many books have been collected.

Some of the books collected by St Joseph's ended up at Tokokoe Library in Ghana, Africa. These children are showing off some of their new books.

Clothes and shoes

Children often grow out of their clothes and shoes while they are still almost new. Do not throw away clothes and shoes that are still in good condition, but are too small for you. There will always be a child somewhere who will be able to make good use of them.

Challenge!

Sort through your clothes.

- Too small? Take them to a secondhand store, give them to a friend or your younger brother or sister.
- Torn? Put them in a pile for mending.
- Stained? Put them in the recycling box.

Mend, alter, and decorate

Before you throw out your old clothes and shoes, see if you can mend, alter, or decorate them and give them a new life. It can be fun. Add a bright, interesting patch to a tear or a hole. Embroider a flower, add ribbons, or pin on badges. Send worn shoes to the shoemaker or buy new laces.

Mend clothes rather than throwing them out and buying new ones.

School uniforms

Does your school have a uniform? If so, yours could be used again and again. Make sure as many children as possible wear your uniform after you have grown out of it. Some charities run uniform recycling programs that help people in poorer countries afford an education.

Eilidh Whiteford, Oxfam's Campaign Manager, in Scotland, says: "Money raised by the sales of recycled school uniforms can help ensure more children receive the right of a free education."

Case study—Friends of Malawi Orphans (FOMO)

A charity called Friends of Malawi Orphans helps children in Malawi, Africa, by providing them with recycled clothes from all over the United Kingdom. FOMO also has its own sewing school in Malawi, where the children are taught to make some parts of their school clothes themselves, teaching them valuable skills for the future.

 **Action!**

Set up a uniform **exchange** or sale at school.

• If you hold a sale you can send the money to buy uniforms so children can go to school in other parts of the world.

FOMO at work

Clothes are collected and packaged up and ready to send to Malawi.

Children are taught how to repair and alter clothes, a valuable skill.

Whole schools are given matching uniforms.

Machines

Fridges, freezers, stoves, washing machines, and dishwashers are called white goods. Every year, mountains of white goods containing dangerous gases are sent to landfills or dumped.

Washing machines and stoves can be recycled and reused rather than dumped.

Old machines

Broken machines can often be repaired. Old machines can be used again by someone else. It is important to get professionals to make sure the machines are absolutely safe before they are reused. If machines are broken, they should be disposed of safely so they do not cause **pollution**.

Challenge!

Find a local organization that sends computers and cell phones abroad.

- Cell phones have a SIM card that can be removed and put into another phone.
- Check that computers and phones are not being handed over with private information still in them.

Action!

Search drawers, toy boxes, and shelves at home and find all the phones you can.

- Ask everyone at your school to do the same.
- Contact a charity that will reuse them responsibly.

A mountain of cell phones lies ready for recycling.

Phones

Cell phones are designed to last up to ten years. They are often replaced after about a year and a half when there is still plenty of life left in them. Charities such as Fonebak reduce the effect of cell phones on the environment by collecting them and sending them to developing countries where they are reused. Broken phones that cannot be mended are recycled responsibly.

Computers

Homes, schools, and businesses all use computers. Computers and software are regularly replaced and updated so equipment that could still have a long and useful life is dumped. Computers are expensive. There are organizations such as Develop Africa, based in the United States, and Computers for Schools, that refurbish, reuse, and donate computers to schools and charities all over the world.

"We are grateful to Computers for Schools, Kenya, for making ICT a reality for the schools in rural Kenya. This initiative will help our young people in the schools and the community at large to acquire the skills needed to thrive in the world of today."

Mr. Yuda, Board of Governors at Karama Secondary School, Meru North, in Kenya, Africa.

Paper

Paper is made from wood. To help the environment, use paper made of wood from forests that can be replanted or use recycled paper. It is even better to use less paper!

The pine trees growing in this plantation have been planted as a crop. They are cut down to be made into paper and new young trees are replanted in their place.

Ancient woodlands

Ancient woodlands are home to a great variety of plants and animals such as these dormice. If trees are cut down to make paper, the animals lose their home. Even if new trees are planted, these create a different kind of **habitat** and many of the plants and animals never return.

Challenge!

Use less paper.
- Think before you print.
- If you do print, use both sides of the paper.
- Write notes on a chalkboard
- Save wrapping paper and use it again.
- Never throw paper away—reuse or recycle it.

Stop junk mail.
- Find out how your home can register to stop receiving junk mail (unwanted mail that is trying to sell something).
- You could put a note on your door or window that says—**NO JUNK MAIL!**

Wood is transported around the world.
This process uses a lot of energy.

Make homemade paper.

This is a good way of reusing paper.

You will need:

- Used paper
- A bowl of warm water
- An egg beater
- A rectangle of fine mesh
- 2 large sheets of blotting paper
- An iron

• Tear the used paper into small pieces.

• Soak the pieces in a bowl of warm water for about ten minutes.

• Beat the mixture with an egg beater to make pulp.

• Lower the mesh into the bowl then lift it out. It should be covered in an even layer of pulp.

• Leave the mesh to drain.

• Turn the layer of pulp onto a sheet of blotting paper.

• Cover it with the other sheet of blotting paper, then iron with a warm iron.

• Lift off the top sheet of blotting paper then leave the pulp to dry for 24 hours. Now use the paper you have made.

Using energy

Wood is often imported, which means it is brought in from another country. Transporting the wood and then making it into paper uses up fuel and causes pollution. Making new paper from old paper uses much less energy.

Waste paper

Paper and cardboard break down in landfills and produce methane, a **greenhouse gas**, that goes into the air and contributes to global warming. Reusing paper helps avoid this.

Action!

Students and teachers can work together to reduce and reuse paper.

Ask your school to only buy recycled paper or paper from renewable forests.

Make a list of all the ways you can reduce your school's use of these paper goods:

• Notebooks

• Toilet paper

• Paper for arts and crafts

Now put your list into action!

Plastic bags

About one trillion plastic bags are used around the world every year. Many bags end up as litter blowing in the wind and floating in the oceans and rivers. Plastic from plastic bags stays in the environment for at least 100 years.

Members of Wonga Beach State School in Queensland, Australia, reduced the number of plastic bags they used and the amount of waste in general.

Case study—Wonga Beach State School

Wonga Beach State School in far north Queensland, Australia, won a prize for cutting down on the amount of plastic bags used in 2007. "Enviro Dollars" were given out to students for reducing waste and for bringing litter-free lunches to school. Recyclable items were also cleaned out and put in the recycling bin. Community businesses donated new items and at the end of the school year the students were able to buy the items with their Enviro Dollars.

Challenge!

Do a plastic bag survey at home.

- How many plastic bags do you have at home?
- How many do you bring home each week?
- How many do you throw away?
- How many do you reuse?
- Can you reduce the number of new plastic bags you use?

A set of Enviro Dollars used by students at the Wonga Beach State School.

Oil

Oil is used to make the plastic used for bags. Reducing and reusing plastic bags will help to save oil, a precious natural resource.

Plastic bags can choke and suffocate people as well as wildlife. Keep them away from young children. Make sure any you use are punctured with small holes to let in air.

Two swans fight over a plastic bag, mistaking it for food.

We depend on oil for fuel and to make plastic, but there is only a limited amount left.

Helping the environment

Reducing the number of plastic bags we use will help keep the environment free of poisonous and dangerous litter. Plastic is a man-made material. It will not biodegrade like natural materials. Plastic bags break down into small, poisonous pieces that end up in the soil, oceans, rivers, and sand where birds and fish accidentally eat them. Plastic bags floating in the sea look like jellyfish, which are food to many sea animals. The animals eat the plastic bags and are poisoned, or choke on them.

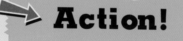 # Action!

Use your old plastic bags to make one big, very strong bag.

- Ask an adult to help you cut plastic bags into strips. Use the strips to knit, crochet, or weave a new strong bag.
- Have a competition at school for the best reused plastic bag design.
- Buy a couple of textile shopping bags and remember to use them instead of asking for a plastic shopping bag.

Disposables

Disposables are things we use and throw away such as diapers, felt-tip pens, paper plates, and styrofoam cups. They are very easy for us to use, but they can cause damage to the environment.

A plastic cup can be reused in all kinds of different ways. It makes a good flower pot. What other ways of reusing it can you think of?

Challenge!

Give up using disposables.
- Before you buy something, ask yourself how many times you will use it. If the answer is you will only use it once, do not buy it!
- If you do buy something that can only be used once, think of a way to reuse it. For example, use plastic cups as plant pots.

Disposable diapers

You may have a baby brother or sister who uses disposable diapers. Disposable diapers contain oil, which is a **raw material**. Energy is also used to make diapers. They are used once, thrown away, and sent to landfills where they take a very long time to break down. Persuade your parents only to buy reusable diapers.

Diapers made of cloth are not disposable. They can be washed and used again and again.

Make your pens last as long as possible. Put the tops back on to stop them from drying out.

Do not use disposable cutlery for picnics. If you have to, wash and reuse them afterward.

Pens

Brightly colored plastic pens are disposable. Once the ink has run out, you throw them away and they go to landfills. Buy refillable pens when you can.

Picnics

Paper and plastic plates, cups, knives, forks, and spoons, and wooden chopsticks are often used once and then thrown away. It saves on washing up, but harms the environment.

⇨ Action!

Think before you pack a picnic or school lunch box.

- Do not use disposable wrapping, cups, plates, napkins, or cutlery.
- Take the right amount of food and there will be nothing to throw away!

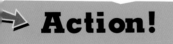

When you pack your school bag, think about what is in it. What can be reused? What will have to be thrown away?

Toys

Toys are fun. They help you to use your imagination and learn new things. You can play with them by yourself or with friends. It is much better for the environment to make your own toys or reuse old ones. Making new toys and games uses up a lot of energy and natural resources.

An old bicycle wheel makes a good hoop to roll along.

Make your own games

Some of the best games need only your imagination. Others can be made from objects lying around the home, with no need to buy anything new. It is easy to make an Oware set like the one opposite. Use an egg carton to make a board of two rows of cells. Then find 48 seeds or beans and put four in each cell. The object of the game is to capture more seeds than your opponent. To find out the rules of the game go to www.wikipedia.org/oware.

This is a traditional Oware board and pieces. Make your own from objects around the house.

Action!

Are you playing with the toys you already have?

- Clean out your toy box.
- Find a new home for toys that you only sometimes or never play with. Give them to charity or to your school sale.
- You can give toys in good condition to a toy library.

Case study—A toy library

Rather than put your toys in a cupboard when you get bored with them, why not let someone else enjoy them? A lot of charities collect toys and games. UNRWA (United Nations Relief and Works Agency) for Palestine Refugees in the Near East is setting up eleven toy libraries in the war-torn Gaza Strip in Israel. About 3,800 children will be able to play with safe toys. The center will also create new opportunities for women, children, and the disabled to join in with their local communities having fun together.

An UNRWA toy library full of second-hand toys ready for children to enjoy.

Batteries

Toys often need batteries to make them work. Batteries are packs of chemicals. When batteries are thrown away the chemicals can leak into the soil. Find out where batteries can be disposed of responsibly. Buy rechargeable batteries that can be reused again and again. Use solar-powered batteries, which are **recharged** by sunlight.

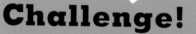

Most electric toys use batteries. Choose rechargeable rather than disposable ones.

Challenge!

Use your imagination.

Some toys can be played with again and again in all kinds of different ways. Try out these toys and games and discover that toys do not have to be expensive to be fun.

- Cards
- Oware/Mancala
- Skipping rope
- Soccer
- Kite
- Dressing up
- Marbles

A green fair

Hold a school fair with a green theme. Invite the local community and share what you have learned about what we can all do to save the planet. You could organize your own green summer fair with a recycling theme.

Green team

One school Green Team had a lot of ideas for their booth. First they held a competition for the best object made from reused materials to be sold at the fair with prizes from a charity. They sold paper weights made from stones, driftwood signs, plants, and flowers grown by the gardening club, and shoe bags and aprons made from reused material.

Amber:
"It was a good idea to get people to reuse their stuff to make stuff."

Emily:
"Re-userific! I liked ... seeing all the things people had made from reusable things. I loved the dream-catcher made from an old piece of wool, corks and see-through plastic paper."

Trafalgar Infant and Junior School's Green Summer Fair got everyone thinking about reducing, reusing, and recycling.

Andy

Paul

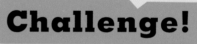

Challenge!

Think up a competition that will encourage everyone at school to reduce and reuse.

How will you judge the winning entry?

Will it be:

- the most original and imaginative idea?
- the idea that makes best use of reusing things?
- the idea that everyone learns the most from?

How can the prize encourage the winner to carry on reducing and reusing?

The House of the Future designs were displayed at the fair so other people could see what the children had learned.

Displays, posters, and pamphlets helped visitors to the Recycle booth learn about how recycling helps protect the environment.

House of the Future Competition

A competition to design a house of the future got the children thinking about eco-friendly materials and waste and energy saving ideas. Some homes already have solar panels to heat water, and wind turbines to make electricity.

Food

The food and drink stalls were planned to create as little garbage as possible. Lunches were sold in brown paper bags that were recycled on the spot. Drinks were served in strong plastic cups that could be washed and reused.

Organizations

Organizations concerned with green issues will usually work with schools to help them learn about how to save the planet and taking action. At this green fair, the local council, Friends of Earth, Fairtrade, and the local Environment Network joined together to set up booths so people could find out about the work they do and get involved.

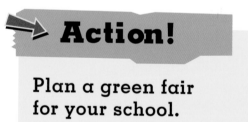

Action!

Plan a green fair for your school.

- How will you encourage people to reduce waste and reuse things?
- What booths will there be?
- What events will you have?
- What food will you serve and how will you serve it?
- Who will you invite?
- What do you hope everyone will learn?
- How do you hope people will change what they do?

Powerful packaging

Urge companies to use less or better packaging.

Let's Get Started!

Many things we buy are packaged in materials like cardboard boxes or plastic wrapping. Some packaging can be recycled. Other packaging cannot. Material that cannot be recycled ends up in landfills. The planet would be cleaner if companies used less packaging. It would also help if they used recyclable or biodegradable material. Biodegradable material breaks down naturally and becomes part of the soil, water, or air.

How can you cut down on the packaging that goes into landfills? One way is to increase awareness. People who buy goods should think about how the goods are packaged. Companies should think about how they package the items they sell.

In this activity, you will explore the packaging of different goods. You will also write a letter to a company. The letter will ask the company to change its packaging.

Activity

Work with a partner to write down answers to the following questions. Then fill in the chart on the next page.

1. Many of the things your family buys are packaged. Soap, shoes, and computer games all come in different kinds of packaging. Why do you think products are packaged the way they are? Does the packaging keep the item protected? Does the packaging help make people want to buy the item?

2. Think of a product that is sold with a lot of packaging. Maybe it is a food item or a toy. Does it need that much material around it to keep it protected? Why do you think it has so much packaging?

Product	Type of Packaging	Reason for Packaging	Recyclable Packaging?
Eggs	Cardboard	Keeps eggs from breaking	Yes

3. Now think of a product that has little or no packaging. Why do you think it is sold like that?

4. What are some types of packaging that are recyclable? Which kinds of packaging would biodegrade? Which kinds would not? Look through the book for reminders.

Looking Back

Choose a product your family often buys that has too much packaging or the wrong kind of packaging. Use the model business letter format on the right to write an email or a letter to the company that makes the product. Find an address for the company on the package or on the internet. Tell the company that your family buys its product. Explain why you would like the company to use less or different packaging. Ask for a reply.

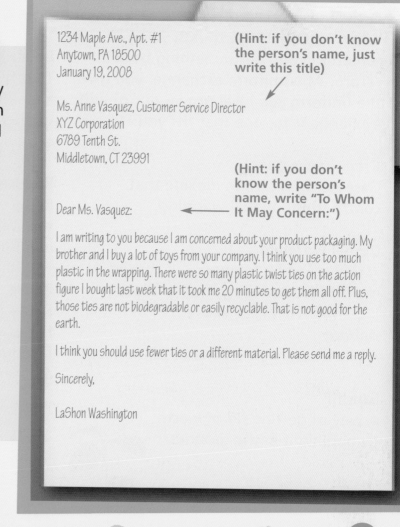

1234 Maple Ave., Apt. #1
Anytown, PA 18500
January 19, 2008

(Hint: if you don't know the person's name, just write this title)

Ms. Anne Vasquez, Customer Service Director
XYZ Corporation
6789 Tenth St.
Middletown, CT 23991

(Hint: if you don't know the person's name, write "To Whom It May Concern:")

Dear Ms. Vasquez:

I am writing to you because I am concerned about your product packaging. My brother and I buy a lot of toys from your company. I think you use too much plastic in the wrapping. There were so many plastic twist ties on the action figure I bought last week that it took me 20 minutes to get them all off. Plus, those ties are not biodegradable or easily recyclable. That is not good for the earth.

I think you should use fewer ties or a different material. Please send me a reply.

Sincerely,

LaShon Washington

Glossary

Biodegradable
When something is biodegradable, it breaks down naturally and becomes part of the soil, water, or air. Vegetable peels are biodegradable but most plastic is not.

Developing country
A developing country is one that is mostly poor but is developing its schools, hospitals, farming, and industry.

Exchange
When you exchange things, you give something and get something back in return. At a uniform exchange, you give the uniform you have grown out of and exchange it for one that fits you.

Greenhouse gas
Gases such as carbon dioxide that contribute to global warming.

Global warming
A rise in Earth's temperature caused mainly by burning oil, gas, and coal.

Habitat
A place where an animal or plant lives.

Landfill
A way of getting rid of waste by burying it in the ground.

Natural resource
Something that is useful to people found in nature such as oil and wood.

Pollution
Pollution is something that harms the natural environment such as air, soil, or water. Exhaust fumes from cars pollute the air. Oil spills at sea pollute the water.

Raw material
A natural material that things are made from, such as cotton, oil, and wood.

Recharge
To refill with energy.
Rechargeable batteries can be refilled with energy when they run out. They can be used again.

Reduce
Reduce means to make less. Reducing the waste we make helps to reduce the amount of garbage going into landfills.

Reuse
Reuse means to use again.
For example, if we reuse plastic bags, it reduces the number being made and sent to landfills.

Websites

www.freecycle.org
More than 4,000 groups of freecyclers across the globe give and get free items by reusing and keeping good items out of landfill sites. Find a group to join near where you live.

www.bookaid.org
Find out how you can donate books and help to give children all over the world the chance to read and learn.

www.oxfam.org
Take your clothes, toys, and other reusable items to an Oxfam shop near you. Money raised will help people all over the world.

www.fomo.co.uk/
Friends of Mulanje Orphans collect clothes and school uniforms to help children in Malawi go to school.

www.eco-shools.org
Your school can become part of an international group of schools committed to caring for the environment.

www.computeraid.org
Instead of throwing usable computers away, find out how they can be reused by schools and businesses in Africa.

www.olliesworld.com
A website for children to learn to reduce, reuse, and recycle.

Note to parents and teachers:
Every effort has been made by the Publishers to ensure that these websites are suitable for children, that they are of the highest educational value, and that they contain no inappropriate or offensive material. However, because of the nature of the Internet, it is impossible to guarantee that the contents of these sites will not be altered. We strongly advise that Internet access is supervised by a responsible adult.

Index

Printed in China